LIVES AND TIMES

Janet and Allan Ahlberg

Wendy Lynch

Heinemann
LIBRARY

First published in Great Britain by Heinemann Library,
Halley Court, Jordan Hill, Oxford OX2 8EJ,
a division of Reed Educational and Professional Publishing Ltd.
Heinemann is a registered trademark of Reed Educational & Professional Publishing Limited.

OXFORD MELBOURNE AUCKLAND
JOHANNESBURG BLANTYRE GABORONE
IBADAN PORTSMOUTH NH (USA) CHICAGO

Designed by Visual Image
Illustrations by Pat Tourret
Originated by Dot Gradations
Printed and bound in Hong Kong/China

05 04 03 02 01
10 9 8 7 6 5 4 3 2 1

ISBN 0 431 02318 2
This title is also available in a hardback library edition (ISBN 0 431 02311 5)

British Library Cataloguing in Publication Data

Lynch, Wendy
Janet and Allan Ahlberg. – (Lives and Times)
1. Ahlberg, Janet – Biography – Juvenile literature
2. Ahlberg, Allan – Biography – Juvenile literature
3. Novelists, English – 20th century – Biography – Juvenile literature 4.
Women novelists, English – 20th century – Biography – Juvenile literature
I. Title
823.9'14
ISBN 0431023182

Acknowledgements

The Publishers would like to thank the following for permission to reproduce photographs: Allan Ahlberg: p22; Chris Honeywell: p8; Yiorgos Nikiteas: pp14, 15, 18, 19, 20, 21 (both), 23; Penguin Books: p17; Telegraph Group plc: p16.

Cover photograph reproduced with permission of Penguin Children's Books.

Every effort has been made to contact copyright holders of any material reproduced in this book. Any omissions will be rectified in subsequent printings if notice is given to the Publisher.

For more information about Heinemann Library books, or to order, please phone ++44 (0)1865 888066, or send a fax to ++44 (0)1865 314091. You can visit our website at www.heinemann.co.uk.

Any words appearing in the text in bold, **like this**, are explained in the Glossary.

Contents

Early life

Allan Ahlberg was born on 5 June 1938 in London. Janet Hall, who became his wife, was born in Yorkshire on 21 October 1944. She grew up in Leicester.

When she was a child, Janet enjoyed drawing. Allan liked to write stories in school and read them to his friends. They both loved to read comics.

Teaching and drawing

Janet and Allan met at **college** in 1962. They were both learning to become teachers. Allan became a primary-school teacher. He loved teaching. Janet decided not to teach.

In 1969, Janet and Allan got married. Janet asked Allan to write a book for children so that she could **illustrate** it. In 1975, *The Brick Street Boys* was **published**.

Words and pictures

Janet and Allan continued working together. Allan wrote the words and Janet drew the pictures. Books like *Cops and Robbers* became very **popular**. Children loved the **rhythm** of the words.

Wicked Witch over the wood
I spy Robin Hood

In 1978, Janet and Allan wrote a book
called *Each Peach Pear Plum*. On each page,
children had to find a **character** from a
fairy tale. The pictures were funny and
full of **detail**.

Happy families

In 1979, Janet and Allan had a daughter called Jessica. Now they began to write books for her. They wrote a **series** of books called *Happy Families*.

Jessica liked to open letters. This gave
Janet and Allan an idea. In 1986, they
wrote *The Jolly Postman*. The book contains
envelopes with letters in them.

Working as a team

Janet liked to listen to the radio as she drew, so she worked in a **studio** above the garage. Allan worked in a quiet shed in the garden. Then they put the words and pictures together.

Janet **suffered** from back pain and this made it hard for her to draw. Allan wrote many more books, but other **illustrators** drew the pictures.

Janet's Last Book

Janet died in 1994. She was only 50 years old. Children and grown ups had loved the **detail** and the fun of her pictures.

ALLAN AHLBERG

JANET'S LAST BOOK

'Janet Ahlberg was most widely known as an
illustrator of children's books, but there was more to her
than that, as you will see – not hear, though, which is
a pity. She had a lovely laugh and did excellent chicken
impressions; clucks, wings and all'

Allan now lives in London but still writes
books for children. In 1996, he wrote
Janet's Last Book as a **tribute** to his wife.

Interviews and photographs

There are a number of ways in which we can find out about Janet and Allan Ahlberg. We can learn about them from **interviews** in newspapers and magazines.

Hitting the jolly jackpot

Picture CAROLINE PENN

The Ahlberg books have become bywords in nurseries and primary schools. **Tiffany Daneff** meets Janet and Allan

THERE cannot be a parent in the country who has not encountered the books of Janet and Allan Ahlberg, the top selling authors for young children. Their books have become bywords in nurseries and primary schools and their rhymes have an uncanny ability to hang around in your head, which is wonderful when children are learning to read and maddening for adults.

Peepo! Each Peach Pear Plum, Funnybones and The Jolly Postman are regularly reprinted, particularly after the Government published its recommended reading list for national curriculum reading tests. This included seven Ahlberg titles among the total of 51 books.

The undisputed best seller, though, has been The Jolly Postman, with more than 125 million hardback copies sold. As with other favourites, the secret of the Jolly Postman's success is fun. It is fun to play with the inserted "letters", the pictures are

Peepo: authors Janet and Allan Ahlberg at home near Leicester – 'they shun publicity and hate having their photograph taken'. Above, their new delivery, The Jolly Christmas Postman

live in the same village, though they have moved to a bigger house overlooking the meadows by the River Soar. Janet and Allan open the door together. He takes the initiative, welcoming me in; she is more shy and reticent.

instantly jolly couple one expects. They are serious about their work and in making every book they produce the very best book possible, from the writing and illustrating down to choosing the right paper and typeface and overseeing the colour printing

other hand he is aware that the publisher wants to produce a book as cheaply as possible. "So there is this tug of war," Allan continues. "They have to put up with it and we have to put up with it and we give ground and accept cer-

every morning with his friends.

Allan tried his hand at radio plays but stopped because he felt he did not have the talent. He went instead to teacher training college where he met Janet. He taught for 12 years,

the form in which I could write." From time to time he tries to write for adults but, he says, that key is not turned

Their first publication was a series of five books called The Brick Street Boys. "They

cake and I gave up teaching," says Allan. But selling the next book was more difficult "I think it took 18 months and about 40 rejection slips," says Allan. They never had an agent and

We can see photographs of Janet and Allan Ahlberg. This is a recent photo of Allan.

Peepo!

We can learn about Allan's childhood by reading and looking at the pictures in a book called *Peepo!* In an **interview**, Allan said, 'I am the Peepo! Baby'.

The pictures in *Peepo!* show you what was
in Allan's house when he was young. Here
you can see a picture of their kitchen.

Books and CD-ROMs

Janet and Allan Ahlberg's books are very **popular**. You can find them in bookshops or in a **library**. There may be some in your school library.

Some of Janet and Allan's books have been made into **CD-ROMs**. You can look at them on a computer. This is a CD-ROM of *The Jolly Post Office*.

Learning about the Ahlbergs

Janet kept all the drawings she did when she was young. We can see these pictures in books. Here is a picture she drew when she was nine.

You can write to the **publishers** of Janet
and Allan Ahlberg's books to learn more
about them. You can also find out more
about them by looking on the **Internet**.

Glossary

This glossary explains difficult words, and helps you to say words which may be hard to say.

CD-ROM shiny disc that can store words, pictures and music

character person in story. You say *ka-rak-ter*.

college place where people go to learn after leaving school

detail small but important part of any whole thing

illustrate draw pictures for books and magazines that make the words easier to understand. You say *ill-us-trayt*.

Internet way in which computers are joined to other computers. You can get information from all over the world.

interview when one person talks to another and what they say is written down or recorded. You say *inter-vue*.

library place full of books. You can often borrow books from a library. You say *lie-bra-ree*.

popular liked by many people

publish when a book is printed and ready to be sold

rhythm the beat in a poem, like music. You say *ri-thum*.

series number of books about the same thing. You say *seer-iz*.

studio room to work in. You say *stew-dee-o*.

suffer feel pain

tribute gift to say thank you to someone who has done something special. You say *trib-yewt*.

Index